D1315999

WHAT DO YOU DO?

JOBS IN YOUR NEIGHBORHOOD

By Emily Perl Kingsley
Illustrated by Tom Cooke

A SESAME STREET/READER'S DIGEST KIDS BOOK

Published by Reader's Digest Young Families, Inc.,
in cooperation with Children's Television Workshop

"I am a farmer. I grow things to eat."

"I am a butcher. I sell lots of meat."

"I am a pilot. I fly jumbo jets."

"I'm a veterinarian. I'm a doctor for pets."

"We build tall buildings, make them higher and higher."

"We are fire fighters. We'll put out the fire."

The crossing guard tells us when it's safe to go.

The baker makes cookies and bread out of dough.

"I'm a mail carrier.
I'll deliver your letter."

"I am a doctor. I'll make you feel better."

"I'm a cashier. I add up what you buy."

"I am a waiter. I serve you your pie."

"I am a dentist. I help keep your teeth strong."

"I am a singer. I'll sing you a song."

"I am a barber. I cut your hair."

"I am a zookeeper. I feed the bear."

"I'm a mechanic. I tow cars when they're stuck."

"I'm a garbage collector. I put trash in my truck."

"I am an engineer, driving a train."

"I am a plumber, unclogging a drain."

"I'm a bus driver. I drive very well."

"I am a teacher. I'll teach you to spell."

"I fix things to eat. I'm called a cook."

"I am a writer. I wrote this book!"